Extreme Cuisine
Slithery, Slimy, Scaly Treats

by Dinah Williams

Consultants:
David George Gordon, author of *The Eat-a-Bug Cookbook*
Andrew Zimmern, co-creator and host of *Bizarre Foods with Andrew Zimmern*

BEARPORT
PUBLISHING

New York, New York

Credits

Cover and Title Page, © John Cancalosi/Alamy; 4L, © William M. Partington, Jr./Photo Researchers, Inc.; 4R, © lonelyplanetimages.com; 5, © Oliver Strewe/lonelyplanetimages.com; 6, © WorldFoto/Alamy; 7, © Zuma/Newscom; 8L, © Graham Day/Photolibrary; 8R, © WaterFrame/Alamy; 9, © Michael Freeman/Corbis; 10, © Claus Meyer/Minden Pictures/Getty Images; 11, © Aaron Nystrom; 12L, © Marco Simoni/Photolibrary; 12R, © Gerald Nowak/Photolibrary; 13, © zunique/Newscom; 14, © Andreas Koschate/Photolibrary; 15, © Riou/photocuisine/Corbis; 16, © David Northcott/Danita Delimont/Alamy; 17, © Christine Kokot/dpa/Landov; 18, © bitis73/ImageVortex; 19, © Maxim Marmur/AFP/Getty Images; 20, © Jeremy Woodhouse/Photolibrary; 21, © Teubner Foodfoto/StockFood Munich; 23TL, © Andreas Koschate/Photolibrary; 23TR, © Brian Weed/Shutterstock; 23C, © Hannamariah/Shutterstock; 23BR, © Gregory Guivarch/Shutterstock; 23BL, © Elke Dennis/Shutterstock; 24, © Dr. Morley Read/Shutterstock.

Publisher: Kenn Goin
Editorial Director: Adam Siegel
Creative Director: Spencer Brinker
Design: Debrah Kaiser
Photo Researcher: Laura Saravia

Library of Congress Cataloging-in-Publication Data

Williams, Dinah.
  Slithery, slimy, scaly treats / by Dinah Williams.
      p. cm. — (Extreme cuisine)
  Includes bibliographical references and index.
  ISBN-13: 978-1-59716-762-8 (lib. binding)
  ISBN-10: 1-59716-762-2 (lib. binding)
  1. Cookery—Juvenile literature. 2. Cookery, International—Juvenile literature.
3. Amphibians—Juvenile literature. I. Title.

TX652.5.W55185 2009
641—dc22
                                        2008036378

For more information, write to Bearport Publishing Company, Inc., 101 Fifth Avenue, Suite 6R, New York, New York 10003. Printed in the United States of America.

10 9 8 7 6 5 4 3 2 1

MENU

Lizard Soup

There's no simple cure for the common cold. To feel better, many people drink orange juice and try to get plenty of rest. In China, however, some people eat lizard soup!

Lizards are a kind of **reptile**. In a part of southern China called Hong Kong, lizards are dried and then boiled in a **broth** with Chinese dates and yams. The cooked lizards are said to taste like fish. To people in some countries, it may seem strange to eat soup that has lizards in it. Yet for a sick person in China, it can seem as natural and soothing as a warm bowl of chicken soup.

lizard

dried lizards

Grilled Iguana

Why are so few green iguanas left in Costa Rica? They taste so good that people are killing—and eating—too many of them!

Green iguanas are large lizards that live in trees. People in parts of Central and South America have been eating them for more than 7,000 years. The tender white meat is often grilled. People say it tastes like chicken. In fact, these lizards are often called "chickens of the trees."

green iguana

grilled iguana

It is against the law to hunt iguanas in Costa Rica. Instead, some farmers raise the animals and sell them for food.

Crocodile Meals

Hungry crocodiles hunt and attack other animals, sometimes even humans, for food. Have hungry people ever hunted crocodiles? Yes. In Papua New Guinea (PAH-poo-ah NOO GIH-nee), villagers have been hunting and eating the fierce reptiles for hundreds of years.

Today, people in Papua New Guinea don't need to go into the wild to catch a crocodile for dinner. The animals are raised on farms and sold around the world—including to fancy restaurants in France. The meat under the reptile's tough skin is easy to cut into steaks, which are perfect for grilling. In Thailand, crocodile meat is used to make a tasty soup.

raw crocodile steak

crocodile

crocodile soup

Many people like the legs and tails from young crocodiles the most. The meat from those parts is very tender.

Turtle Shell Stew

People usually serve **stew** on a plate or in a bowl—but not in the **rain forests** of Peru. Villagers there use a large turtle shell to hold their food. What's inside? It's turtle meat stew, of course.

To make the dish, hunters first catch a giant river turtle and cut off its shell. They clean and salt the shell and place it over hot coals. Next, the turtle meat is placed inside. Mashed bananas, sweet peppers, onions, and spices are also added. Once the food is cooked, the shell holds a tasty stew called *sarapatera*.

giant river turtle

turtle stew

turtle shell

People in Peru
have been making
turtle stew for at
least 600 years.

Raw Sea Turtle Eggs

Sea turtles have few enemies in the ocean. On land, however, they aren't so lucky. Some people in Nicaragua like to eat the eggs that turtles lay in the sand.

Sea turtle eggs look like boiled Ping-Pong balls. The large sea reptiles can lay up to 200 eggs at a time. To eat them, people make a small tear in the soft shells, add a little hot sauce, and suck down the raw eggs. They feel slimy and taste a bit fishy, but to those who like them they make an "egg-cellent" meal!

green sea turtles

turtle eggs
being collected

Sea turtles are in
danger of becoming extinct.
One reason is that too many
people are eating their eggs. As a
result, many countries have passed
laws that make it illegal to
collect sea turtle eggs.

Frogs' Legs

People in France love eating frogs' legs so much that the small **amphibians** almost became extinct there. Too many were being killed for food. Today, it's against the law to kill frogs in France. Instead, frogs' legs are shipped there from other countries, such as Indonesia.

To make the popular French dish, a cook seasons a frog's large back legs with onions, parsley, garlic, and lemon juice. Then the cook dips the legs in batter and fries them in olive oil. Frogs' legs can also be cooked in butter. Lemon juice and parsley are later sprinkled on top. People say frog meat tastes like a combination of fish and chicken.

fried frogs' legs

Frogs' legs are also eaten in many other countries, including Italy, China, Spain, and the United States.

Barbecued Frogs

Frogs' legs on a menu may seem unusual enough, but what about the rest of the frog? Do people eat that, too? In Thailand, some people eat the whole frog. To cook it, they barbecue the animal over a fire. It may look burned, but it's not. Some people sell these crunchy treats in markets. Customers can then bring the barbecued frogs home and eat them with rice.

In the Philippines, large frogs are skinned, hollowed out, and stuffed with chopped pork. The stuffed frogs are then fried in hot oil and eaten.

barbecued frog

Snake Blood Drinks

Some snakes can kill a person. In parts of Asia, however, it's the other way around. People kill snakes—so that they can drink their blood!

Some restaurants in China, Thailand, and Malaysia keep live snakes on hand so that they can make a drink from the snakes' blood. Sometimes the blood is mixed with water. Other times people just drink it plain. Some people believe that drinking snake blood keeps them healthy.

cobra

Snake blood drinks can be made from the blood of cobras.

snake blood

19

Rattlesnake Chili

Dead animals don't bite. Or do they? Some rattlesnakes have bitten a person hours after being killed! That's why people in Texas and in other parts of America's Southwest are very careful when they make rattlesnake chili. The first thing they do is cut off the snake's head and put it in a closed container. Next, they skin the reptile. To remove its bones, they boil the animal's body in water and lemon juice. The meat is then ready to be cooked in a large pot with beans, tomatoes, and hot peppers. This chili is a spicy dish that has a real bite to it!

rattlesnake chili

Snake meat is also a popular food in parts of China. One restaurant in Guangzhou (gwahng-JOH), a city in southern China, has 75 different snake dishes on its menu.

Where Are They Eaten?

Here are some of the places where
the slithery, slimy, scaly treats in this book are eaten.

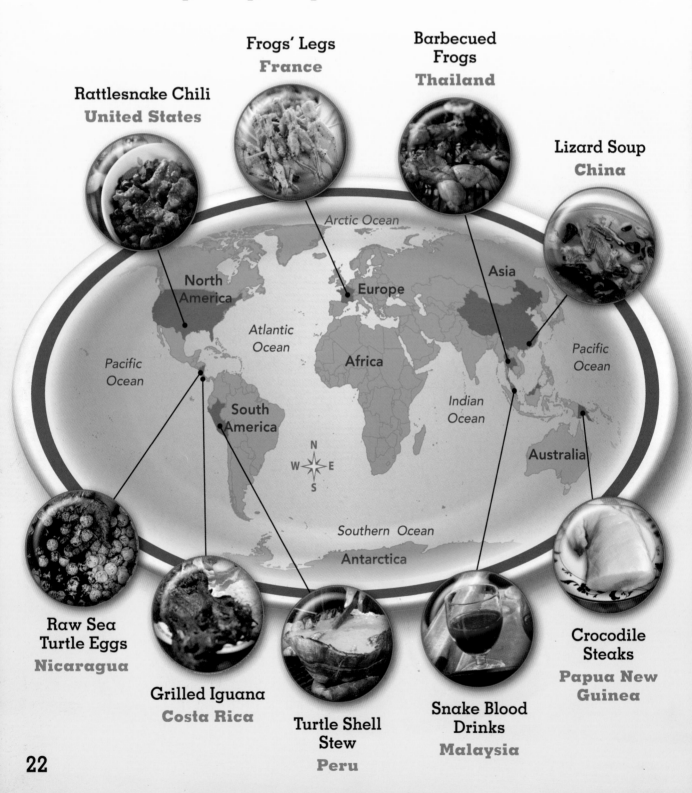

Frogs' Legs
France

Barbecued Frogs
Thailand

Rattlesnake Chili
United States

Lizard Soup
China

Arctic Ocean

North America

Europe

Asia

Atlantic Ocean

Africa

Pacific Ocean

Indian Ocean

Pacific Ocean

South America

Australia

N W E S

Southern Ocean

Antarctica

Raw Sea Turtle Eggs
Nicaragua

Grilled Iguana
Costa Rica

Turtle Shell Stew
Peru

Snake Blood Drinks
Malaysia

Crocodile Steaks
Papua New Guinea

Glossary

amphibians (am-FIB-ee-uhnz) cold-blooded animals, such as frogs, toads, and salamanders, that have a backbone and live part of their lives in water and part on land

broth (BRAWTH) the liquid that meat or vegetables are boiled in

rain forests (RAYN FOR-ists) wet places where it rains very often and lots of trees and plants grow

reptile (REP-tile) a cold-blooded animal, such as a lizard, snake, turtle, or crocodile, that has dry, scaly skin, a backbone, and lungs for breathing

stew (STOO) a thick soup-like dish, usually made with meat and vegetables

Index

Bibliography

Hopkins, Jerry. *Extreme Cuisine: The Weird & Wonderful Foods That People Eat.* London: Bloomsbury (2004).

Schwabe, Calvin W. *Unmentionable Cuisine.* Charlottesville, VA: University Press of Virginia (1994).

Read More

Platt, Richard. *They Ate What?!: The Weird History of Food.* Minnetonka, MN: Two-Can Publishing (2006).

Wishinsky, Frieda, and Elizabeth MacLeod. *Everything but the Kitchen Sink: Weird Stuff You Didn't Know About Food.* New York: Scholastic (2008).

Learn More Online

To learn more about slithery, slimy, scaly foods, visit
www.bearportpublishing.com/ExtremeCuisine

About the Author

Dinah Williams has edited and written many books for children.
She has also eaten many weird meals. She lives in Cranford, New Jersey.